Rediscovering the Validity and Importance
of the Solemn League and Covenant

THE ANGLOSPHERE'S BROKEN
COVENANT

Rediscovering the Validity and Importance
of the Solemn League and Covenant

THE ANGLOSPHERE'S BROKEN
COVENANT

MICHAEL WAGNER

cántaro
publications

cántaro
publications

www.cantaroinstitute.org

The Anglosphere's Broken Covenant: Rediscovering the Validity and Importance of the Solemn League and Covenant
by Michael Wagner

Published by Cántaro Publications, a publishing imprint of the Cántaro Institute, Jordan Station, ON.

Book design by Steven R. Martins

Library & Archives Canada

ISBN 978-1-990771-16-3

Printed in the United States of America

TABLE OF CONTENTS

PREFACE

I WAS FIRST confronted with the possibility that the Solemn League and Covenant was still binding upon Britain and its former colonies in 1995. I would have read of that Covenant in books before 1995, but the view that it was binding upon Christians presently in some sense never occurred to me in the slightest before hearing of the "Covenanter" position.

I spent a lot of time and effort investigating the Covenanter claims. The more I studied, the more compelling those claims appeared to be. As years went by, and I continued to look at it from various angles, I had fewer and fewer doubts that the Solemn League and Covenant was still binding. From the theological, historical and philosophical perspectives, the Covenanter position is solid.

Ultimately, it became unfathomable to me that such an important event — Britain making a covenant with God — would become generally forgotten by the English-speaking peoples. How could this event be so widely ignored? Indeed, Bible-believing Christians, of whom there are many in the English-speaking countries, seemed especially ignorant of the Covenant when it should have been a cornerstone of their historical knowledge. How the mighty have fallen. Where are the Christian leaders who should have been informing their flocks about this covenant and its obligations?

I am convinced that knowledge of the Solemn League and Covenant and its obligations will become widespread in the future. For this to happen, people will need to hear about it and read about it once again. It is my hope that this short book will contribute to a reawakening of interest in the Solemn League and Covenant and its implications.

Michael Wagner
Edmonton, Alberta, Canada
June 2010

1

INTRODUCTION

WITH THE PASSAGE of time many important events begin to fade from people's memories. This seems to be the case with us as individuals but also as nations or societies. Although some very significant historical events remain etched in our consciences today, such as World War Two and the Holocaust, other events become forgotten, only to be studied by historians. This is probably a natural phenomenon as we struggle to deal with current problems rather than remaining fixed on the past.

It may be unreasonable to expect people to know much history. But a basic knowledge of key historical events is necessary to understand one's own society. Thus, public and private education programs generally include some amount of historical study. This suggests that the value of knowing history is generally recognized.

What history do people really need to know? The founding of their country? The great wars? The historical oppression of minorities? Even among historians there are differences of opinion about what is most important for people to learn. Events that are not considered to be important or relevant are more likely to be left out. No one can know everything about history, so choices must be made about what to study.

I would like to suggest that one of the most important historical events in the history of the English-speaking nations has been widely forgotten. In 1643 the three nations of Britain, England, Scotland and Ireland (apparently Wales was considered to be within the confines of England at the time) made a covenant with God, the triune God of the Bible. Britain covenanted with God after the pattern of Israel in the Old Testament. This is a major historical event that has been forgotten, and it has significant implications for our day. The covenanting nations, and the other English-speaking nations that would be subsequently formed by people from these nations, are still bound in covenant to God. Their having forgotten the covenant does not lessen their bonds to the Lord. These nations are under God's judgment for their covenant-breaking.

What is a covenant? "A covenant is a mutual engagement between two parties, implying the performance of certain duties on the one hand, and the fulfillment of promises on the other. In religious covenants, God and His people are the parties" (Houston 1857, 13). The historic British people, in the widest sense, are parties to a covenant with God, the Solemn League and Covenant of 1643.

The purpose of this little book is to reawaken people in Britain and the British settler nations (Canada, Australia, New Zealand and the USA) to their covenant ties to the Lord God of the Bible. Yes, this is the Christian God, the God of Abraham, Isaac and Jacob. I'm not talking about "god" in a general sense that all religions share together. I'm not talking about Allah or Buddha or any of the other false gods of the world. The Covenant was with a specific God, the only true God, Jehovah.

A recent term used to describe English-speaking civilization is the "Anglosphere." In its core sense, this term refers to Britain and the nations founded by settlers from Britain. The British settler nations share with their mother country a language, culture, political tradition, and I would argue, covenant obligations to God.

The book begins by providing a brief look at the Biblical argument for nations covenanting with God in modern times, that is, the practice of "national covenanting." Largely forgotten today, the ordinance of national covenanting was widely accepted by the Protestants of the sixteenth and seventeenth centuries.

Next, the book looks at the historical situation leading to the swearing of the Solemn League and Covenant. The Solemn League and Covenant was formulated within a particular historical situation. But it was a covenant with the Lord made by the English Parliament and other significant authorities in Britain. The nation was bound to God in a perpetually binding covenant. Subsequently, the governing British authorities repealed the Solemn League and Covenant, and it has been officially ignored since that time.

But an oath sworn to God cannot actually be repealed; God does not release people from their lawful vows to Him. The book thus provides argumentation for the continuing validity of the Covenant bonds sworn in 1643.

Finally, the book argues that not only Britain, but also the British settler nations (the Anglosphere) are bound by the Covenant. Canada, Australia, and New Zealand still have strong constitutional ties to the British monarchy. Although the United States currently has no such ties, an examination of early American history demonstrates that it was founded by people bound by the Solemn League and Covenant. Those bonds do not evaporate over time, and so the United States remains under those covenant obligations.

It is my hope that by raising awareness about this forgotten Covenant, and its obligations on the peoples of the English-speaking nations, that people will turn to the Lord with their whole hearts and a revival of God's truth will spread across these nations. May it be so.

2

NATIONAL COVENANTING IN THE BIBLE

IN TIMES OF REVIVAL in the Old Testament, God's people would often covenant together to follow Him with all of their heart. These covenant renewals were frequently led by Israel's political leader of the time, namely, the king.

One of these revivals, leading to Judah making a national covenant with God, occurs in 2 Chronicles chapter 15. The prophet Azariah gave a message from the Spirit of God to Judah's king, Asa. The central component of the message was, "The LORD is with you, while ye be with him; and if ye seek him, he will be fond of you; but if ye forsake him, he will forsake you" (verse 2). Verse 8 then notes that Asa "took courage" from the words of the Lord, cleansed the land of idols and "renewed the altar of the LORD." The people of Judah saw that God was with Asa and gathered themselves together in a special kind of revival meeting. 2 Chronicles 15:10-15 records what happened next as follows:

> So they gathered themselves together at Jerusalem in the third month, in the fifteenth year of the reign of Asa. And they offered unto the LORD the same time, of the spoil which they had brought, seven hundred oxen and seven thousand sheep. And they entered into a covenant to seek the LORD God of their fathers with all their heart and with all their soul; That whosoever would not seek the LORD God of Israel should be put to death, whether small or great, whether man or woman. And they sware unto the LORD with a loud voice, and with shouting, and with trumpets, and with cornets. And all Judah rejoiced at the oath: for they had sworn with all their heart, and sought him with their whole desire; and he was fond of them: and the LORD gave them rest round about.

All of the people, the whole nation, swore a covenant to follow the Lord with their whole heart.

A similar kind of revival broke out under King Josiah of Judah. Josiah became king when he was quite young. The Bible says that in the eighth year of his reign, "he began to seek after the God of David his father" (2 Chronicles 34:3). He subsequently began to cleanse the land of idolatry, rebuild the house of the Lord, and take the Scriptures (which had been recovered by Hilkiah the priest) very seriously. Subsequently, the Lord sent a message that Josiah would be rewarded with peace during his reign. Josiah then gathered the nation together to make a covenant with the Lord, as recorded in 2 Chronicles 34:29-33:

> Then the king sent and gathered together all the elders of Judah and Jerusalem. And the king went up into the house of the LORD, and all the men of Judah, and the inhabitants of Jerusalem, and the priests, and the Levites, and all the people, great and small: and he read in their ears all the words of the book of the covenant that was found in the house of the LORD. And the king stood in his place, and made a covenant before the LORD, to walk after the LORD, and to keep his commandments, and his testimonies, and his statutes, with all his heart, and with all his soul, to perform the words of the covenant which are written in this book. And he caused all that were present in Jerusalem and Benjamin to stand to it. And the inhabitants of Jerusalem did according to the covenant of God, the God of their fathers. And Josiah took away all the abominations out of all the countries that pertained to the children of Israel, and made all that were present in Israel to serve,

even to serve the LORD their God. And all his days they departed not from following the LORD, the God of their fathers.

Josiah made the covenant himself and also caused all of his subjects "to stand to" the covenant as well. The whole nation was in covenant with the Lord.

In the sixteenth and seventeenth centuries, it was a common view among Protestants that these kinds of national covenants could be made by Christian countries as well. The covenanting that occurred in the Old Testament among God's people in their national capacity was believed to provide a pattern that could be followed by nations in the New Testament Christian dispensation.

Archibald Mason, a Presbyterian minister of the late eighteenth century, wrote a treatise providing the theological argumentation in favor of national covenanting. After citing examples of Old Testament covenanting mentioned above, as well as others, he continues as follows:

> These scriptures plainly prove that God's covenant with Israel was made with them, in their public national capacity. It was not made with one of the tribes, or with some individuals in all the tribes; but it was with the whole body of the people that this covenant was made, and to all of them its obligation extended. The covenanting, therefore, that is warranted, in the days of the

gospel, to be carried on in Christian lands, may and ought to be transacted by them, in their public national character. It is not lawful for a few persons in a land only, when they come to be enlightened in the knowledge of the gospel, and have been determined to embrace it, to join themselves to the Lord in a perpetual covenant; but it is lawful for a people, in their national state, when they are brought to the knowledge or profession of the truth, to do the same thing. Since covenanting with God was a moral duty, incumbent upon his people, under the former dispensation, and was performed by them in their national character; it certainly must be the duty of the Christian church, when the Lord in his goodness brings her in any land unto a national form, to practice this moral duty in their public capacity (Mason [1799] 2002, 37).

Some people will undoubtedly point out that God's people in the Old Testament constituted a theocracy and were therefore in a unique position. Their circumstances were different in this respect from the New Testament people of God, and therefore following their practice of national covenanting today is not valid. But Mason, like the earlier Reformed and Presbyterian theologians, rejected that line of argument:

When a nation is enlightened with the gospel, comes to receive the truths of Christ, makes a profession of his religion, and submits to his ordinances and laws, it is as much a theocracy, a people under the immediate and

13

gracious government of God, and are as much bound, by covenanting nationally with him, to swear an oath of national allegiance unto the Lord, as ever the house of Israel and the house of Judah were to perform this service in the land of Canaan (Mason [1799] 2002, 42-43).

Of course, much more could be said in defence of the ordinance of national covenanting. Mason wrote a book defending the practice, and other Presbyterian theologians have written in defence of it as well. The point here is just to provide a glimpse of the Scriptural case for national covenanting as background information.

There is a strong Scriptural argument for national covenanting. It was so strong, in fact, that England, Scotland and Ireland would make such a covenant with God in 1643. Previously, Scotland had made its own national covenant with God in 1581 and it would renew that covenant in a time of major crisis in 1638. The ordinance of national covenanting with God is forgotten in our day, but in the English-speaking countries of the seventeenth century, it was widely recognized and clearly held to be valid.

3

THE SOLEMN LEAGUE
AND COVENANT

IN THE FIRST YEARS of the early church, various kinds of man-made doctrines and practices began to appear among Christians. Doctrinal battles over vital issues raged during this period, and the victories of the Bible-believing Christians led to what are known as the "ecumenical creeds" which define the boundaries of orthodoxy for all Christians. However, as time went on, some man-made doctrines and practices gradually became dominant, and by the Middle Ages the church had in many respects become corrupt.

While some groups of Christians resisted these corruptions (led by men such as John Wycliffe and John

Hus), the most significant effort to purge out the dross began with Martin Luther in 1517. Luther's efforts to reform the church quickly spread throughout northern and western Europe. The Frenchman John Calvin soon became a leading Reformer, based in Geneva. And one of Calvin's disciples, John Knox, was unquestionably the leading Reformer in Scotland.

Under Knox's leadership, Scotland became a Presbyterian country. The Church of Scotland became an established church. A national covenant for that nation, involving both the church and the state, was made with God in 1581, the National Covenant of Scotland.

The Stuart kings in the first half of the seventeenth century, James I and Charles I, were not happy with Presbyterianism. The representative form of government involved in Presbyterianism did not fit well with the Stuarts' absolutist views. James famously said, "No bishop, no King," fearing that the lack of a hierarchy in Presbyterianism would lead to a decline in royal power. The monarch was considered to be the head of the church in the episcopal form of government of the Church of England. Charles I wanted to be the acting head of the Church of Scotland as well.

Unfortunately for Charles, his efforts to force episcopal forms of worship upon the Church of Scotland in 1637 backfired. The Presbyterian people of Scotland completely rejected Charles' prayer book. The National Covenant of Scotland was updated and renewed in

1638, in the midst of a national spiritual awakening, and a major aspect of the covenant renewal was the rejection of episcopal government and worship. This was the beginning of what is called the "Second Reformation," being a reformation from the man-made religion favored by a despotic king and his royalist supporters.

Charles then twice attempted to force Scotland into subjection by military might, but on both occasions the Scots raised substantial armies for defense of their nation and covenant, and Charles backed down.

By this time Charles was also having problems in England. The House of Commons was dominated by Puritans, who, like the Presbyterians in Scotland, believed that the church should be conformed to Biblical patterns under Christ, rather than being subjected to the rule of the king. They also rejected the king's claim to a virtually absolute political authority. Ultimately, the English Civil War broke out in 1642 between the King and his supporters on one side, and the Parliament and its supporters on the other.

The English Parliament and the nation of Scotland were natural allies in this conflict. Both had suffered from the dictatorial ambitions of King Charles. Thus the English Parliament asked Scotland to make a formal league—a military alliance—against Charles. Scotland was agreeable to that idea as long as it included a specifically religious bond aiming at a uniformity of Biblical doctrine and practice among the British churches.

The resulting political and religious document, a league and covenant between England, Scotland, Ireland and God, was the Solemn League and Covenant.

In the meantime, the English Parliament had already convened an important gathering of England's top theologians to determine how to reform the Church of England to conform it to Biblical doctrine and practice. The existing episcopal system of church government would be replaced by Biblical church government, as determined by these theologians. This multi-year conference took place at Westminster and was known as the Westminster Assembly.

The Solemn League and Covenant was drafted by Rev. Alexander Henderson on behalf of the Church of Scotland and subsequently sent to England for approval.

> The covenant was then transmitted to the English Parliament and the Westminster Assembly; and being, with some slight alterations, approved by them, it was appointed to be taken on the 25th of September. On that memorable day, the members of the House of Commons, with the Assembly of Divines, and the Scottish Commissioners, met in the Church of St. Margaret's, Westminster. The Rev. Mr. White, of Dorchester, one of the Assessors, commenced with prayer. Alexander Henderson and Mr. Nye afterwards addressed the assembly, justifying from Scripture the practice of covenanting, and showing its manifold advantages to the Church in

all ages. Mr. Nye then read the Covenant from the pulpit slowly, and aloud, pausing at the end of each article, while the whole audience of statesmen and divines stood up reverently to worship, and with uplifted hands swore to its performance. After prayer, at the close, the members of the House of Commons subscribed their names to the covenant in one roll of parchment, and the Assembly of Divines in another. The covenant was taken by the House of Lords, on the 15th of October, after a sermon by Dr. Temple, from Nehemiah x. 29, and an exhortation by Mr. Coleman. On the following Lord's day, it was also taken by the congregations in and around London. In the month of February following, the Parliament ordained that the covenant should be taken throughout the kingdom of England, by all persons, who had sufficient knowledge, above the age of eighteen years. This order was accompanied by a suitable Exhortation of the Westminster Assembly. Both were sent to military officers, that it might be taken by the soldiers under their command—to governors of towns and garrisons—to committees of Parliament in the several counties, and to ministers and churchwardens, that it might be read and explained to the people. It was ordered to be publicly read in every church and congregation in the kingdom, on every day of public fasting and humiliation. English Protestants residing in foreign countries were invited to join with their brethren in England in this sacred league; and not only they, but also some of the Continental Churches expressed their readiness to comply with this invitation. These orders did not require the power of public authority to enforce them; as it is acknowledged, even by historians unfriendly to the principles of the covenant, that "the great majority of the religious part of the nation were zealous for the covenant."

In Scotland, the Solemn League and Covenant was received with the highest approval, and cordial unanimity. . . . Printed copies were sent to the moderator of every presbytery; and it was ordered that it should be received and explained on the Sabbath, and then, on a subsequent Sabbath, tendered to the people. Throughout the kingdom, it was everywhere received with fasting and prayer, and embraced with the utmost unanimity. In 1644, it was ratified by act of Parliament; and it was again renewed in Scotland, by all ranks, at the close of the Second Reformation, with an Acknowledgment of sins, and Engagement to duties, in 1648, and by the Scottish Parliament in 1649 (Houston 1857, 52-54).

The embrace of the Solemn League and Covenant was not quite as widespread in Ireland as it was in England and Scotland, but it was nevertheless embraced by that nation. John Brown quotes one source as noting, "the English Parliament by an ordinance enjoined that covenant to be taken in Ireland; and accordingly it was sworn by almost all the Protestants in Ulster, who acknowledged the authority of the Parliament, the greatest part of the Protestants in Ireland all concurred in it" (Brown [1803] 2010, 116-117). In sum, from looking at various sources Brown concluded, "it appears, that the body of Protestants in Ireland took the Solemn League and Covenant" (Brown [1803] 2010, 117).

The point here is that England, Scotland and Ireland covenanted with each other and with God to, among other things, preserve the Presbyterian Church of Scotland and to reform the churches of England and Ireland according to the Word of God, the Bible. These nations were formally in covenant with God. Since God is a party to the covenant, only He can release these nations (and any other nations it binds) from the terms of the covenant. He has not done so.

The taking of the Solemn League and Covenant was a major event of international significance in 1643. However, it wasn't long before powerful forces were at work to undermine the covenant. Charles II, the eldest son of Charles I, would play a central role in trying to overturn the Solemn League and Covenant.

4

THE DEMISE OF THE SOLEMN LEAGUE AND COVENANT

SCOTLAND AND THE English Parliamentary forces won the war against Charles I. He surrendered to the Scottish army, who then turned him over to the English. The English Parliament tried him for treason and then executed him.

The Scots were not pleased by this regicide. They still supported the monarchy; they just didn't want a despotic king who claimed to be head of the church and deprived his people of their rightful liberties. Thus, they offered the throne to Charles' eldest son, provided that he would take the Solemn League and Covenant.

He agreed, and was crowned king in January, 1651.

> While the oath of office was being administered, the prince kneeled in apparent humility, and lifted up his right hand in a solemn appeal to God. At this point he uttered the awful vow in the presence of the people: "By the Eternal and Almighty God, who liveth and reigneth forever, I shall observe and keep all that is contained in this oath." He also said: "I will have no enemies, but the enemies of the Covenant—no friends, but the friends of the Covenant." Thus King Charles II. became a radical Covenanter by profession and protestation in the most solemn manner (McFeeters 1913, 147).

Having made Charles II king, the Scots were now on a collision course with the English Parliament which had passed a law making it treason to proclaim the executed king's son to be the new king. In short, a war broke out and the English Parliamentary forces, under the command of Oliver Cromwell, defeated the Scots. Charles II could not assume the throne in Britain yet. As well, in the confusion of defeat, the Church of Scotland began to divide between strict supporters of the covenants and those who took a more liberal approach.

Cromwell became the ruler of Britain, but he died in 1658. After a brief interlude, Charles II was received as king in 1660. This is known as the "Restoration" because the British monarchy was restored after Cromwell's crypto-republican rule.

Although Charles II had received his crown from the Scots on the condition of embracing the Solemn League and Covenant, upon achieving power he immediately went to work to overturn the Covenant. He had only taken the Covenant as a ploy to gain power. His vows were false. He was a great deceiver.

The Sedition Act of 1661 declared the Solemn League and Covenant to be null and void. Then in 1662, the Act of Uniformity was adopted, forcing all ministers to implement man-made liturgies in worship services. As a result, the "Great Ejection" took place whereby all faithful Bible-believing ministers were forced out of their churches in Britain for their failure to conform to Charles II's proposed idolatry. About 2,000 pastors in England and 400 in Scotland were ejected for their unwillingness to adopt government-sponsored forms of worship.

From here it was all downhill. In Scotland, thousands of people chose to hear the preaching of the ejected ministers out in the fields rather than attend the churches of the government's official pastors. "The king sent detachments of his army over the country to compel the people, who had lost their pastors, to attend services under the ministers of the Episcopal Church. They refused" (McFeeters 1913, 198).

The government took ever sterner measures to prevent people from attending the field meetings rather than attending the government churches. Ultimately, attending a field meeting became punishable by imprisonment or death. Those who refused the government churches and remained faithful to the Solemn League and Covenant were called "Covenanters." To make a long story short, the Covenanters resisted King Charles II and his successor James II, and justified their resistance as loyalty to the Covenant. Persecution of the Covenanters became incredibly severe, and most were eliminated either by death or by surrender to the king's terms.

James II was so evil, however, that the majority of people in England and Scotland rose up against him and supported William, Prince of Orange from the Netherlands, James' son-in-law, as a replacement king. Thus in the Glorious Revolution of 1688, James was overthrown and his wicked persecution of God's people came to an end. The government of Britain could now be placed on a more agreeable basis than an absolute royal tyranny.

The new governmental situation of Britain after William's triumph is known as the Revolution Settlement. It was much better than governance under the Stuart kings, of course, but it too ignored the terms of the Solemn League and Covenant. "The Settlement of 1688 failed to recognise the Solemn League and Covenant by which these lands had plighted [sworn] their faith to God. It not only disregarded that bond but grossly violated its obligations and set them at nought" (M'Donald 1881, 96).

A point by point examination of how the Revolution Settlement violated the Solemn League and Covenant would be quite lengthy and even tedious. However, one point that most people can easily understand and sympathize with is that the Revolution Settlement maintained the British monarch as head of the Church of England. This clearly violated the Solemn League and Covenant.

> The Settlement of 1643 contemplated and secured the spiritual independence of the Church and her freedom from all civil control. The Settlement of 1688 established the very opposite. An ecclesiastical hierarchy cannot be without its head, its *pontifex maximus*, to whose determination all matters of chief importance must be referred, and whose judgment is final. This office of surpassing arrogance the Church of Rome assigns to the Pope, but the Episcopal Church and the British nation assign it to the Queen. It was precisely this office that was claimed by the Stuarts. Wrested at first from the Pope by Henry VIII., and by the Parliament of 1538 conferred upon him, it has been held and its power has been exercised by all the Kings and Queens that have sat on the British throne to the present day—not, it is true, invariably with the same energy, but as far as the law is concerned, with equal authority. Queen Victoria is as much the head of the Church in 1880, as King Henry VIII. was in 1538 (M'Donald 1881, 97-98).

Under the Solemn League and Covenant the monarch would not be the head of the church. Only Christ can be the Head of His church. Making a government official the head of the church is blatantly unscriptural and violates the oath that the British government made with God. There are other important elements of the Revolution Settlement that violate the Solemn League and Covenant as well, but this point should be clear to all.

Since that time the Solemn League and Covenant has been ignored by government officials (as well as most Christians generally) in Britain. But ignoring it does not make its obligations disappear. Ignorance of the law does not excuse anyone, and deliberately ignoring an obligation is even worse than not being aware of a law. Despite its exclusion from the Revolution Settlement, the Solemn League and Covenant is still binding upon Britain and the nations that have descended from Britain.

5

THE CONTINUING OBLIGATION OF THE SOLEMN LEAGUE AND COVENANT

JUST BECAUSE BRITAIN has officially ignored the Solemn League and Covenant since the Glorious Revolution of 1688 does not mean that God has released Britain from the terms of the Covenant. God has not released Britain and its daughter nations from the Covenant.

Britain bound herself to God by oath as strongly as any nation could possibly be bound.

The solemn deed of 1643 was, moreover, as we have seen, in the fullest sense of the term, a national transaction, seeing that it was signed not merely by a pleni-potentiary, but also by the rulers of the nation, and by the great mass of the people themselves. But even more than that, it was not only signed, but confirmed by an appeal to God—by solemn oath. The national faith was thus plighted [sworn] by all the means through which a nation is accustomed to express its mind, and no nation, no matter in what way it may choose to make its voice heard, and no matter what be the object for which it has voluntarily given its pledge, ever could be more firmly bound than was the British nation by the transaction of 1643. All this being so, it is not possible for any people to be more solemnly bound by the engagements of their ancestors, or to have more weighty obligations resting upon them to implement those engagements, than is the case with the British nation at the present time. And if ever any obligation, arising out of a national trans-action, descended from one generation to another, the obligations of that Solemn League and Covenant must rest upon this present generation with all their accumu-lated weight (M'Donald 1881, 72-73).

This is a point worth emphasizing. It wasn't just a small group of fanatics who covenanted with God. Indeed, it wasn't just the Church of England and the Church of Scotland that made this Covenant. The Cov-enant was made by the collective national governments of the British Isles in their full governing capacity.

These covenants were strictly NATIONAL DEEDS, and on this ground they are of perpetual obligation upon the British nation. The supreme authorities in Church and State entered into them—the people of all ranks willingly and joyfully came under the engagement. They became part of the fundamental compact between the ruler and the subject; and were assumed, after solemn and careful deliberation, not only as the ground of international union, and mutual protection and intercourse, but likewise as the basis of national legislation and administration. If the British nation be morally the same society that came under these engagements, then it is certainly yet bound to carry out the ends which they proposed, and that until these shall have been fully attained. If righteous laws bind posterity—if oaths are binding—if bonds oblige heirs—if compacts are of force while the national society exists,—then assuredly the British covenants have a continued obligation, and that of a higher and more sacred character than any laws and compacts which pertain merely to worldly interests and relations (Houston 1857, 69).

Governments make significant and perpetually binding decisions at times and no one challenges their right to do so. Governments bind themselves in constitutions to treat their citizens in certain ways. When a government violates a term of its constitution in its treatment of a citizen, there is often outrage among the population. If a government is expected to honor such commitments to their citizens, surely it must honor any commitments it has made to God.

> The engagements of rulers to a people, or of a people to their rulers—as in the Magna Carta, and the Bill of Rights,—are held to be of fundamental, permanent obligation; and certainly, the covenant by which both rulers and people are not only mutually bound to one another, but also to Him who is moral Governor of the nations, and Prince of the kings of the earth, can plead a still higher obligation. It is universally admitted that a righteous league between nation and nation is binding; and while the breach of international treaties is held to be perfidious and criminal, is there not aggravated sin in a nation breaking its covenant with God? Before the permanent obligation of the British Covenants can be set aside, objectors will require to show that the nation is not possessed of a permanent moral identity—or, admitting this, that it is not still bound by its own just engagements. But such an identity and obligation can only be denied by repudiating, at the same time, all public faith, and by maintaining that no bonds or treaties whatever bind posterity (Houston 1857, 69-70).

Some may argue that the Solemn League and Covenant was repealed by the British government in 1661 and therefore it is no longer valid. The British government made the Covenant, so it has equal authority to undo its own work. The problem with this argument is that God is one of the parties to the Covenant, and He does not recognize any attempt to withdraw from legitimate obligations made to Him.

> The allegation that the Covenants, National and Solemn League, were rejected by the nation at the Restoration, by the Act Rescissory, and that they have ceased to be obligatory—on the principle that the authority which enacted a law, may afterwards repeal it, is of no weight with those who consider properly the circumstances of the case, or who have due regard to Scriptural precedent. In the covenants of our illustrious forefathers, the exalted Mediator—the Head of the nation, was one of the contracting parties; and He can never give to a people a right to dispense with the obligation of solemn duties enjoined in His Word (Houston 1857, 70-71).

Just because we have not been taught about the Solemn League and Covenant does not mean we are released from our obligations under it.

> Although a covenanted people may so far forget and disown their special relation unto God, as neither to be sensible of their voluntary obligation unto him, nor seek or expect covenant-blessings from him; yet the Lord will not in this manner, nor on that account, give up with his interest in, or relation unto them. What the Lord did for his people Israel, he will do, in his own time and way, for every Christian covenanted land (Mason [1799] 2002, 60).

33

Indeed, and once our ignorance of the Covenant is overcome, our opposition to it doesn't do us any good either. Disliking the Covenant does not relieve us of our obligations under its terms.

> Ignorance of the nature of these covenants, of their obligation upon us, or of the duties to which we are bound by them, cannot relieve our souls from their binding force. No enmity at these solemn deeds can deliver the consciences of those who hate them from their obligation. No contempt and reproach, which we may pour upon our national vows, will avail to set loose from the duties thereof, those who have their mouths filled with hard speeches against them. Neither can any practical contradiction of them, or apostasy from them, set us free from their obligation (Mason [1799] 2002, 69).

Despite the fact that the vast majority of people in the English-speaking world have been ignorant of the Solemn League and Covenant for decades, if not centuries, God still holds us accountable to it. The Anglosphere nations are guilty of covenant-breaking before Almighty God. It's time to return to the Lord.

Some people may be stumbled by certain phrases in the Solemn League and Covenant that refer to specific circumstances of mid-seventeenth century Britain. If those circumstances have changed (and they have), then perhaps the Covenant is no longer binding. But any change in circumstances cannot alter a covenant to obey God. There may be ways in which the fulfilling of covenant obligations are affected by changing circumstances, but the overall bond with the Lord is not dissolved.

For example, the Covenant obliges its swearers to promote the king's well-being. But even in Britain itself there is no king right now (but rather a queen). So is that obligation null and void? No. It was clearly the intent of the Covenant's original framers to have the Covenant apply to the succeeding British monarchs as well as the sitting monarch of the time. So the idea of promoting the king's well-being means the well-being of any subsequent lawful ruler as well. This can be accomplished by people in any land with a lawful government.

The issue of circumstantial terminology is similar in the Canadian Constitution. As we will see in the next chapter, the Canadian Constitution vests the executive power in the Queen. This part of the Constitution was written in 1867 when Victoria was the Queen. So it was referring to Queen Victoria. But, of course, she died and was followed by her son, Edward VII. The Constitution did not need to be amended to replace the word "Queen" with the word "King." It was taken for granted that the Constitution's vesting of the executive power in the Queen would apply to her successors. Even though the circumstances change, the words of the Constitution remain the same and the obligations are basically the same as well.

Thus when the Solemn League and Covenant refers to the king, it is most reasonable to think of it as applying to him and his successors, not just to him alone. Similarly, although the Covenant refers most specifically to the three kingdoms of England, Scotland and Ireland, it also applies to the nations that descended from them, not just those specific nations.

The case for the continuing obligation of the Covenant on the British Isles is easy to understand, since the nations of those Isles are specifically mentioned in the Covenant. But the nations founded by settlers from the British Isles are also bound.

When a group of Englishmen, for example, settled in North America, their Covenant bonds to the Lord were not dissolved just because the colony they now lived in was not a geographical part of England. It was still constitutionally part of England in the sense that it was ruled by the English government and the settlers enjoyed the rights of Englishmen. And this is a very important point. How could settlers in North America claim to have the rights of Englishmen unless they were in a real sense English citizens under the English Constitution?

6

THE ANGLOSPHERE NATIONS ARE BOUND BY THE SOLEMN LEAGUE AND COVENANT

ENGLAND, SCOTLAND AND Ireland swore the Solemn League and Covenant. These countries now constitute the United Kingdom and the Republic of Ireland. But they are not the only countries bound by the Solemn League and Covenant. How could that be? How could nations that did not exist when the Solemn League and Covenant was taken be bound by it?

It's rather simple, actually. People in Britain, who were unquestionably bound by the Solemn League and Covenant, left Britain and founded new nations. When these settlers left the British Isles and crossed the sea, their covenant bonds to God went with them. Those bonds did not disappear just because they left the confines of the original covenant nations. They were bound to God in covenant while in Britain, and they were still bound to God in covenant after they left Britain because their relationship with God is not a function of geography. Covenant-bound people founded new nations; those new nations are also bound by the same covenant. They have the same covenant DNA as the original nations that swore the covenant.

In this respect, all of the core nations of English-speaking civilization, the Anglosphere if you will, are bound by the Solemn League and Covenant. The British settler countries still reflect the influence of their British founding in a myriad of ways. Canada, Australia, and New Zealand maintain clear constitutional ties to the British monarchy, for example. And although the United States does not have such clear constitutional ties, there can be no denying the essential British influence in its formation.

The Anglosphere

The term "Anglosphere" was coined rather recently to describe the entirety of English-speaking civilization. I think this term can be helpful to describe the nations that are still bound by the Solemn League and Covenant. The main theorist behind the Anglosphere concept is James C. Bennett. He says it is helpful to think of the Anglosphere idea "as concentric spheres marked by differing degrees of sharing of the core Anglosphere characteristics" (Bennett 2007, 80). The innermost sphere contains the nations originally populated by British settlers which subsequently assimilated immigrants from other countries into the English-speaking, common law culture. "This core group includes the United States, the United Kingdom, Ireland, Australia, New Zealand, English-speaking Canada, and the English-speaking Caribbean, along with assorted small islands and territories" (Bennett 2007, 81).

The "middle" part of the Anglosphere consists of nations where English is one of the principal languages, but where other languages are also important. A number of countries in Africa (former British colonies) fit into this category as does the Philippines.

The "outer" part of the Anglosphere is where English is one of the major languages, but the nations primarily identify themselves with another major civilization tradition, not the Anglosphere. India, Pakistan, and some Arab states fall into this category, for example.

It seems to me that the "core group" of the Anglosphere consists of those nations bound by the Solemn League and Covenant. It is possible that other former

British colonies (such as India) should also be considered as being bound by it, but I am not making that argument here. I am just focusing on the British settler nations which are certainly still bound. This is the core group of the Anglosphere, although for my purposes I'm not addressing the Caribbean nations and small islands that Bennett also suggests are in the core group.

Bennett provides more detail in describing the Anglosphere as follows:

> To be part of the Anglosphere implies the sharing of fundamental customs and values at the core of English-speaking cultures: individualism; rule of law; honoring of covenants; in general, the high-trust characteristics described by Francis Fukuyama in *Trust: The Social Virtues and the Creation of Prosperity*; and the emphasis on freedom as a political and cultural value. The Anglosphere shares a narrative in which the Magna Carta, Bill of Rights, trial by jury, "innocent until proven guilty," "a man's home is his castle," and "a man's word is his bond" are common themes (Bennett 2007, 79-80).

The core group of the Anglosphere shares the political inheritance of Britain, which as Bennett notes above, includes the Magna Carta and English Bill of Rights. The political traditions of the United States are all part of this Anglosphere inheritance. "The American Constitution is not self-sufficient but exists embedded in a wider unwritten constitutional tradition of custom and common law shared with Britain and the rest of the Anglosphere" (Bennett 2007, 181).

Indeed, the legal tradition of the common law is one of the most important characteristics that the Anglosphere nations share.

> A business lawyer from any common-law nation can understand the basics of any other common-law code. The differences among American states, English law, and Canadian and Australian codes mean that most Anglosphere lawyers already have a feeling for the variability among the different codes. He or she will know the basic outlines of the problem before he begins work and is used to talking with lawyers expert in the codes of other common-law jurisdictions (Bennett 2007, 181).

The core group of the Anglosphere is in a real sense all part of a common culture and civilization. This is not surprising because they all have the same origins in people from the British Isles. The people of the British Isles—that is, the people who originally bound themselves to God in the Solemn League and Covenant—left their homeland to found the United States, Canada, Australia, and New Zealand. When they left their homeland they did not leave their language, culture, political philosophy, or religious obligations behind. All of those things came along with the British settlers. Subsequent historical events did not release these people and their descendants from their religious bonds to the Lord.

The core nations of the Anglosphere have the same basic language, the same basic culture, the same basic political philosophy, and—I would argue—the same covenant obligations to God. Being a part of the core of the Anglosphere includes all of these things. And none of the Anglosphere nations have made any attempt to keep their covenant with the Lord. They are all covenant-breaking nations.

Canada's British Connection

When the American War of Independence ended, many of the colonists who remained loyal to Britain left the newly independent United States. Thousands flocked to the remaining British colonies north of the new country. Thus the northern most part of the continent remained loyal to Britain and ultimately formed Canada. The British North American colonies became the independent nation of Canada in 1867, but Canada maintained strong political, cultural and constitutional connections with Britain for many years. Some of those connections remain today.

The strong cultural ties can probably be said to have lasted at least until the 1960s. All of the Western nations experienced social upheavals during the 1960s, and Canada was no exception. The most famous literary manifestation of English-speaking Canadian nationalism, George Grant's *Lament for a Nation*, is largely an expression of regret that Canada was rapidly losing its

Britishness and becoming more Americanized.

In contrasting Canada and the United States, Grant noted the significance of Canada's British connection:

> English-speaking Canadians had never broken with their origins in Western Europe. Many of them had continuing connections with the British Isles, which in the nineteenth century still had ways of life from before the age of progress. That we never broke with Great Britain is often said to prove that we are not a nation but a colony. But the great politicians who believed in this connection—from Joseph Howe and Robert Baldwin to Sir John A. Macdonald and Sir Robert Borden, and indeed to John G. Diefenbaker himself—make a long list. They did not see it this way, but rather as a relation to the font of constitutional government in the British Crown. Many Canadians saw it as a means of preserving at every level of our life—religious, educational, political, social — certain forms of existence that distinguish us from the United States (Grant [1965] 2005, 70).

Many English-speaking Canadians held strong feelings of attachment to Britain, even those who were not necessarily ethnically British, with Prime Minister John Diefenbaker being a perfect example. Indeed, as Leader of the Opposition in 1964, Diefenbaker led the fight to preserve Canada's older flag, the Red Ensign (which included the Union Jack in the upper left corner) against Prime Minister Lester Pearson's new maple leaf flag (known unaffectionately by some conservatives as the "Pearson Pennant").

Adopting the new flag was seen by many Canadian conservatives as a deliberate rejection of Canada's British connection, in a sense a rejection of Canada's history. The prestigious historian, Donald Creighton, expressed this view when commenting on the maple leaf flag as proposed by a government committee:

> The new flag, with its deliberate rejection of Canada's history and its British and French legacies, bore a disturbingly close resemblance to the flag of a new 'instant' African nation, a nation without a past, and with a highly uncertain future. The exclusive reliance on the maple leaf, an heraldic symbol appropriate only to a national or provincial shield or escutcheon, revealed the committee's, and the government's, poverty of invention, and their total failure to provide effective substitutes for the historical traditions they had summarily dismissed (Creighton 1970, 337).

The point here is that the introduction of the new flag was resisted as representing a break with Canada's historical connection to Britain.

Canada's Constitution

Canada's ties to Britain are more than just historical, however. Even a cursory reading of this country's constitution makes the ties between the two nations extremely vivid. The preamble to Canada's constitution (the Constitution Act, 1867) begins as follows: "Whereas the Provinces of Canada, Nova Scotia, and New Brunswick have expressed their Desire to be federally united into One Dominion under the Crown of the United Kingdom of Great Britain and Ireland, with a Constitution similar in Principle to that of the United Kingdom: And whereas such a Union would conduce to the Welfare of the Provinces and promote the Interests of the British Empire . . . " The constitutional connection, through the British Crown at least, is very clear from that statement.

But there's more. Under the section on Executive Power in the Constitution, the following is stated: "The Executive Government and Authority of and over Canada is hereby declared to continue and be vested in the Queen." Not only that, but "The Command-in-Chief of the Land and Naval Militia, and of all Naval and Military Forces, of and in Canada, is hereby declared to continue and be vested in the Queen." This is the current authoritative Constitution of Canada. The British monarch holds the power of the executive branch of the Canadian government, and he or she is also the commander in chief of the Canadian Armed Forces. Of course, in practice the Queen doesn't exercise these powers nowadays, but they are still firmly entrenched in the current constitution. Thus there remains an explicit constitutional connection between Canada and the British Crown. The connection to the Crown is important because the British Crown was one of the parties to the Solemn League and Covenant.

Australia's Constitution

Like Canada, Australia is a British settler nation that has maintained its historic ties to Britain to a significant degree. This fact is reflected in that country's constitution. The preamble to Australia's constitution (Commonwealth of Australia Constitution Act, 1900) begins much like Canada's: "WHEREAS the people of New South Wales, Victoria, South Australia, Queensland, and Tasmania, humbly relying on the blessing of Almighty God, have agreed to unite in one indissoluble Federal Commonwealth under the Crown of the United Kingdom of Great Britain and Ireland, and under the Constitution hereby established . . . " Shortly after the preamble is the statement, "The provisions of this Act referring to the Queen shall extend to Her Majesty's heirs and successors in the sovereignty of the United Kingdom."

Also, like Canada's constitution, the reigning British monarch holds the executive power: "The executive power of the Commonwealth is vested in the Queen and is exercisable by the Governor-General as the Queen's representative, and extends to the execution and maintenance of this Constitution, and of the laws of the Commonwealth." The command of Australia's military is held on behalf of the reigning British monarch: "The command in chief of the naval and military forces of the Commonwealth is vested in the Governor-General as the Queen's representative."

Hence there remains a strong constitutional link between Australia and the British Crown, which as noted earlier, was one of the parties to the Solemn League and Covenant.

New Zealand's Constitution

New Zealand has a so-called "unwritten" constitution, so it's in a somewhat different constitutional situation than Canada and Australia. Nevertheless, much like those other two nations, there is enough authoritative legislation to demonstrate the continuing constitutional link between New Zealand and the British Crown.

The following should be noted from New Zealand's Constitution Act 1986. Section 2 of the Act concerns the Head of State. It states that "(1) The Sovereign in right of New Zealand is the head of State of New Zealand, and shall be known by the royal style and titles proclaimed from time to time. (2) The Governor-General appointed by the Sovereign is the Sovereign's representative in New Zealand." We know that the Sovereign referred to here is the reigning British monarch because Section 5 of the Act is entitled Demise of the Crown and reads as follows:

> (1) The death of the Sovereign shall have the effect of transferring all the functions, duties, powers, authorities, rights, privileges, and dignities belonging to the Crown to the Sovereign's successor, as determined in

accordance with the enactment of the Parliament of England intituled The Act of Settlement (12 & 13 Will. 3, c. 2) and any other law relating to the succession to the Throne, but shall otherwise have no effect in law for any purpose.

(2) Every reference to the Sovereign in any document or instrument in force on or after the commencement of this Act shall, unless the context otherwise requires, be deemed to include a reference to the Sovereign's heirs and successors.

Clearly, New Zealand is constitutionally bound to the British Crown. Although the statements in New Zealand's Constitution Act 1986 regarding the Crown aren't quite as blatant as the Canadian and Australian constitutions, the ties are nevertheless unmistakable.

America's British Connection

Although the United States does not currently have direct constitutional links to Britain like Canada, Australia, and New Zealand, it is nevertheless bound by the Solemn League and Covenant. The community that would become the United States of America was founded by British settlers who themselves were bound by the Covenant. Thus, even when that community became independent of Britain, the covenant bonds with God remained. God did not release the early Americans from their covenant obligations just because they broke their ties to Britain.

In one of his last books, the great American scholar Russell Kirk described the strong historical linkage between Britain and the United States. There were four specific areas where he noted the inseparableness of these two great nations. The United States had received from Britain its language and culture, its system of law, its representative political institutions, and its concepts of morality and character.

> In 1620, the English Pilgrims settled at Plymouth, in what is now Massachusetts. In language and literature, Virginia and Massachusetts (and presently eleven other colonies) transplanted England to the eastern shore of America. Almost four centuries later, that language and that literature remain the footing for the culture of some two hundred and eighty million North Americans (Kirk 1993, 21).

Culturally, the American settlers were one with the British. More accurately, they were British. Kirk notes that "Right down to the fighting at Lexington, Concord, and Boston in 1775, Americans looked to London, Edinburgh, and Dublin for literary and philosophical judgments" (Kirk 1993, 23). He also quotes another scholar as pointing out that during the first 150 years of settlement, Americans "envisioned in America a projection of English civilization" (Kirk 1993, 24). Culturally, America and Britain were one.

Just as American culture is an outgrowth of British

culture, so also is American law the outgrowth of British law. The settlers in the American colonies brought with them the English common law, and after their independence they maintained the common law. In fact, those who fought for American independence appealed to their rights under common law to justify their political claims.

> The Patriots were asserting their claim to enjoy what Edmund Burke called "the chartered rights of Englishmen"—not the abstract claims of perfect liberty that would be asserted fifteen years later by French revolutionaries. Rooted in custom and ancient usage, the Common Law's purpose was to work for social harmony, not for social revolution. The American Revolution did not sever the links between British law and American law; rather, the American Republic added more chapters to the complex history of common law (Kirk 1993, 34).

What is the origin of American law? Did it arise from American soil on its own? No. American law was originally transplanted British law.

Related to this, and yet distinct, is the American form of representative government. The early colonies had representative forms of government and upon independence retained representative government. The pattern of representative government was inherited from Britain. The Americans adapted the specific governmental institutions to their own situation, but the principle of representative government came from Britain. The local colonial governments "enacted legislation much as they pleased, claiming that they were entitled to enjoy across the Atlantic all the chartered rights of Englishmen" (Kirk 1993, 53). Representative government in the United States "is an inheritance from British political experience and usage" (Kirk 1993, 47).

Finally, the moral traditions, habits and manners of the United States are British in origin. This is largely due to the fact that the American settlers brought their religion with them from Britain. There were a number of different churches and sects that appeared in the American colonies. But despite their differences,

> all read King James's Bible (with the exception of the Catholics, who had the Douay Bible); all preached the theological virtues of faith, hope, and charity. All spoke and read English, all lived under English law, all abided by many old English prescriptions and usages. Theirs was Christianity in British forms (Kirk 1993, 71).

My point here, of course, is that the early American colonies were a transplanted part of Britain. Britain was under the Solemn League and Covenant, and so its transplanted colonies were also under the same covenant. Kirk notes in a couple of places that the American settlers claimed to have the "rights of Englishmen." This is only possible for people who live under English rule, under the English constitution. How otherwise could they have the rights of Englishmen? How could they have the rights of Englishmen without any of the duties of Englishmen? They were Englishmen in a constitutional sense. And thus they were (and their descendants are) bound by the Solemn League and Covenant.

It is worth mentioning that when the colonies became independent they did not lose those bonds. The covenant is with God, and by breaking their connection to Britain the Americans did not break free from their bonds to God. The United States is still bound by the Solemn League and Covenant.

Immigrants or Settlers?

The United States has been described as a "nation of immigrants." In a sense, this is not really true. The United States (as well as Canada, Australia and New Zealand) are not "immigrant countries" but "settler countries," and there is an important difference. Immigrants move from one country to another country. Settlers move from one country to a new territory where they found a new nation. The four nations listed above fall into this second category of settler countries. They were all settled and established by the British. Immigrants only came after the nations were already established in some sense. This distinction has been made by the political scientist, Samuel P. Huntington.

Huntington also corrects the perception that America was founded in the late 1700s.

Americans commonly refer to those who produced independence and the Constitution in the 1770s and 1780s as the Founding Fathers. Before there could be Founding Fathers, however, there were founding settlers. America did not begin in 1775, 1776, or 1787. It began with the first settler communities of 1607, 1620, and 1630. What happened in the 1770s and 1780s was rooted in and a product of the Anglo-American Protestant society and culture that had developed over the intervening one and a half centuries (Huntington 2005, 40).

Speaking of the colonies at the time of the War for Independence, Huntington points out that "In terms of race, ethnicity, culture, and language, Americans and British were one people" (Huntington 2004, 47). One of the major lines of reasoning that the colonists used to justify their struggle for independence was

that the British government was itself deviating from English concepts of liberty, law, and government by consent. Americans were defending these traditional English values against the efforts of the British government to subvert them. "It was a resistance," Benjamin Franklin said, "in favor of a British constitution, which every Englishman might share . . . a resistance in favor of the liberties of England" (Huntington 2005, 47).

Here again we see that the American colonists considered themselves entitled to English constitutional rights. They knew they were under the English constitution. That being the case, they were surely bound by the Solemn League and Covenant (which lawfully became a part of the English constitution in 1643 and which no man could annul or repeal because the Covenant was made directly with God Himself).

Admittedly, the argument for the United States being bound by the Solemn League and Covenant is not as simple as the argument for the other core Anglosphere nations. Those other nations have direct constitutional ties to the British monarchy, whereas the United States does not. Nevertheless, it is still unmistakable that the early British settlers "transplanted England to the eastern shore of America," in the words of Russell Kirk quoted above. A transplanted covenanted nation is still a covenanted nation.

The American War of Independence did not break the covenant bonds between the Lord and the people of the thirteen colonies. It broke the political and constitutional ties with Britain, of course. But that is not sufficient to break the covenant ties with God. The United States was originally founded by people from a nation that made an explicit covenant with God. Independence from Britain broke the ties with that nation but could not break the obligations to God.

Conclusion

Britain made an explicit covenant with God, and it is thus easy to see that Britain is still bound by that covenant. In subsequent years some covenant-bound British people traveled overseas to settle and found new nations. They carried their covenant obligations with them. The new nations that were founded are thus basically under the same covenant obligations as the mother country.

The continuing ties to Britain are easy to see with regard to Canada, Australia, and New Zealand. The constitutions of these countries make those ties as plain as can be. The national flags of those latter two nations contain the British Union Jack in the upper left corner. Until 1965, Canada's national flag also had the Union Jack in the upper left corner. Until this very day the provincial flags of the Canadian provinces of Manitoba and Ontario still have the Union Jack in the upper left corner. The provincial flag of British Columbia contains the Union Jack stretched across its entire upper segment. The British connection cannot be missed.

The situation of the United States is a little bit trickier because the British connection is not as blatant as the other core Anglosphere nations. Nevertheless, for those who have eyes to see, the British founding of America deposited the covenant DNA of the mother country, and that DNA cannot be erased by time or nationalistic sentiments. Looking at the early history of the American settlements reveals the unmistakable imprint of the British constitution and probably every other aspect of British political, cultural, and religious life. Like Britain, Canada, Australia, and New Zealand, the United States of America is bound by the Solemn League and Covenant.

7

CONCLUSION

READERS MAY or may not be convinced by the information and arguments presented in this book. There's
a wise old saying, "don't believe everything you read."
It's good to take a critical stance when presented with
a different perspective, especially one that may seem
so different from the norm. Take some time to think
through the information and to consult other sources
of information. Check it out. You don't need to jump
to conclusions.

Did Britain really make a covenant with God in
1643? Read some mainstream historical sources on seventeenth century Britain. Why was the covenant subsequently ignored, especially after the Glorious Revolution of 1688? Were there good reasons to consider the

Solemn League and Covenant null and void? Or was it just easier to sweep it under the rug?

I am thoroughly convinced that the information and argumentation presented in the preceding chapters is true. I'm so convinced, in fact, that I want to encourage people to carefully scrutinize this perspective in light of history and theology. Some of my history may be off; some of my arguments may be invalid. Maybe my presentation of the Covenanter position is weak. There's plenty of material now available in conventional books and on the Web to provide a corrective to any errors of fact or reasoning that I may have made. I'm not trying to fool anybody. Find out for yourself.

If I'm right, then the Anglosphere nations have much to account for. They need to repent of their covenant-breaking and return to the Lord. I hope this happens, and I believe it will happen. That will be a great time of revival and reformation. May that time come soon.

Benefits of the Solemn League and Covenant

Despite over three centuries of covenant-breaking, the Anglosphere nations have nevertheless reaped benefits from their special relationship with the Lord. It is true that they are under God's judgment, but He is also very merciful to them. He has not forgotten the covenant bonds.

Thomas Houston, writing in the 1850s, points out that Biblical Christianity was more vigorous in the covenanted nations than in any other nations. This is probably still true today.

> It is a circumstance worthy of particular observation, that in those countries where the profession of Divine truth was ratified, and secured by solemn scriptural vows, true religion has been preserved, and political liberty has been transmitted from one age to another, much better than in places where social covenanting was unknown. Revivals of scriptural principle, too, in our day, have occurred more in the former countries than in the latter (Houston 1857, 10).

It is commonly observed that evangelical Christianity is more vigorous in the United States than in any other country. To lesser degrees the other core Anglosphere nations also have vibrant evangelical communities. Some people will undoubtedly (and rightly) point out that there are significant weaknesses in the modern evangelical movement. Nevertheless, the Bible is taken seriously as the Word of God among the evangelical communities, and as a result, the Bible is probably taken more seriously in the Anglosphere countries than in any other countries of the world.

Besides the lingering spiritual benefits that Houston attributes to the Solemn League and Covenant, he also argues that it has played a significant role in the tradition of civil liberty enjoyed by the Anglosphere nations.

The Third Article of the Solemn League plainly implies that the people have a right to appoint rulers, and prescribe the conditions of government, according to the will of God; that no rulers should be chosen who are not friendly to true religion; and that the supreme ruler is bound to respect and maintain the constitutional liberties of the nation. Civil liberty was regarded as founded on and inseparable from religious purity and freedom; and the basis of both was declared to be the word of God. The king was to be amenable to the authority of the enthroned Mediator; while the subjection and civil duties of the people were to be regulated in accordance with His revealed will. In these fundamental principles, so briefly but yet so clearly enunciated, are contained the germs of all true and permanent liberty; and it is not too much to say, that to the Solemn League and Covenant, Britain and America are largely indebted for the constitutional freedom which they possess above other nations (Houston 1857, 62-63).

It is thus arguable that the Solemn League and Covenant has played a role in making the Anglosphere nations the freest nations in the world.

Furthermore, from a Christian perspective, the taking of the Solemn League and Covenant in 1643 represents the high-water mark of godly civil government in world history.

The Reformation of 1643 extended to the State as well

as to the Church. The standard of God's Word was applied to the civil affairs of the nation. The throne, the legislative assembly, and the bench of justice, were all shielded with the utmost care by wholesome legislative enactments, securing that all profane persons, and such as were the enemies of religion, should be excluded from places of power and trust. The nation thus practically, in the highest and noblest sense of the terms, did homage to Christ as Prince of the kings of the earth, and as Governor among the nations (M'Donald 1881, 74).

Probably no nation has ever attained to such a conscious degree of Christianization as Britain had in 1643. And since the other core Anglosphere nations are off-shoots of Britain, they share in this godly heritage. They do not live up to this heritage, of course, but neither can they escape it.

The period of the Second Reformation was thus the bright spot in British history. Then the noble attempt was made by the reformers to bring the nation into subjection to Christ. Then the nation both in its individual members and its institutions was more in harmony with the will of God as revealed in His Word than ever before or since. Then the Sabbath was respected, and profanity and immorality checked. Then the worship of God in the family was universal, and integrity and truth characterized the intercourse of man with man (M'Donald 1881, 75).

What a wonderful situation. A whole nation bound in covenant with God and following His Word. This seems almost unfathomable in our day and age. But it is the true heritage of Britain—and Canada—and Australia—and New Zealand—and the United States. Does this not make you yearn for these backsliding nations to return to the Lord? God has not forgotten the Solemn League and Covenant.

Rediscovering the history and importance of the Solemn League and Covenant is no small task. And to do so basically involves starting from scratch. On the one hand, that sounds discouraging. On the other hand, starting from such a very low point is often how God likes to do things, so that it will clearly be His work, not the successful efforts of some person or organization. He alone will receive all the glory.

Think about this information and pray about it. If it's totally off the wall, you have nothing to worry about. On the other hand, if this information is true, you do have something to worry about. Your own relationship with God, not to mention the well-being of your family, church, and nation, is at stake. Look to the Lord for guidance about this matter. He will not lead you wrong.

REFERENCES

Bennett, James C. 2007. *The Anglosphere Challenge: Why the English-Speaking Nations Will Lead the Way in the Twenty-First Century*. Lanham, MD: Rowman & Littlefield Publishers.

Brown, John. [1803] 2010. *A Refutation of Religious Pluralism*. Lewiston, ID: Gospel Covenant Publications.

Creighton, Donald. 1970. *Canada's First Century*. Toronto: Macmillan of Canada.

Grant, George. [1965] 2005. *Lament for a Nation*. Montreal & Kingston: McGill-Queen's University Press.

Houston, Thomas. 1857. *A Memorial of Covenanting*. Paisley: Alex. Gardner.

Huntington, Samuel P. 2005. *Who Are We? The Challenges to America's National Identity*. New York: Simon & Schuster Paperbacks.

Kirk, Russell. 1993. *America's British Culture*. New Brunswick, NJ: Transaction Publishers.

Mason, Archibald. [1799] 2002. *Observations on the Public Covenants, Betwixt God and the Church. A Discourse.* York, PA: Covenanted Reformed Presbyterian Church.

M'Donald, John. 1881. *Jehovah-Nissi: The Lord My Banner, Or, The Lord's Banner as Displayed in the British Isles at the Reformation, and still upheld by the Reformed Presbyterian Church.* Glasgow: Thomas Smith & Co.

McFeeters, J. C. 1913. *Sketches of the Covenanters.* Philadelphia.

APPENDIX

THE SOLEMN LEAGUE AND COVENANT

A SOLEMN LEAGUE AND covenant for Reformation and Defence of Religion, the honour and happiness of the King, and the peace and safety of the three kingdoms of England, Scotland and Ireland.

We noblemen, barons, knights, gentlemen, citizens, burgesses, ministers of the Gospel, and commons of all sorts in the kingdoms of England, Scotland and Ireland, by the providence of God living under one King, and being of one reformed religion; having before our eyes the glory of God, and the advancement of the kingdom of our Lord and Saviour Jesus Christ, the honour and happiness of the King's Majesty and his posterity, and the true public liberty, safety and peace of the kingdoms, wherein every one's private condition is included; and calling to mind the treacherous and bloody plots, conspiracies, attempts and practices of the enemies of God against the true religion and professors thereof in all places, especially in these three kingdoms, ever since the reformation of religion; and how much their rage, power and presumption are of late, and at this time increased and exercised, whereof the deplorable estate of the Church and kingdom of Ireland, the distressed estate of the Church and kingdom of England, and the dangerous estate of the Church and kingdom of Scotland, are present and public testimonies: we have (now at last) after other means of supplication, remonstrance, protestations and sufferings, for the preservation of ourselves and our religion from utter ruin and destruction, according to the commendable practice of these kingdoms in former times, and the example of God's people in other nations, after mature deliberation, resolved and determined to enter into a mutual and solemn league and covenant, wherein we all subscribe, and each one of us for himself, with our hands lifted up to the most high God, do swear,

I.

That we shall sincerely, really and constantly, through the grace of God, endeavour in our several places and callings, the preservation of the reformed religion in the Church of Scotland, in doctrine, worship, discipline and government, against our common enemies; the reformation of religion in the kingdoms of England and Ireland, in doctrine, worship, discipline and government, according to the Word of God, and the example of the best reformed Churches; and we shall endeavour to bring the Churches of God in the three kingdoms to the nearest conjunction and uniformity in religion, confession of faith, form of Church government, directory for worship and catechising, that we, and our posterity after us, may, as brethren, live in faith and love, and the Lord may delight to dwell in the midst of us.

II.

That we shall in like manner, without respect of persons, endeavour the extirpation of Popery, prelacy (that is, Church government by Archbishops, Bishops, their Chancellors and Commissaries, Deans, Deans and Chapters, Archdeacons, and all other ecclesiastical officers depending on that hierarchy), superstition, heresy, schism, profaneness, and whatsoever shall be found to be contrary to sound doctrine and the power of godliness lest we partake in other men's sins, and thereby be in danger to receive of their plagues; and that the Lord may be one, and His name one in the three kingdoms.

III.

We shall with the same sincerity, reality and constancy, in our several vocations, endeavour with our estates and lives mutually to preserve the rights and privileges of the Parliaments, and the liberties of the kingdoms, and to preserve and defend the King's Majesty's person and authority, in the preservation and defence of the true religion and liberties of the kingdoms, that the world may bear witness with our consciences of our loyalty, and that we have no thoughts or intentions to diminish His Majesty's just power and greatness.

IV.

We shall also with all faithfulness endeavour the discovery of all such as have been or shall be incendiaries, malignants or evil instruments, by hindering the reformation of religion, dividing the King from his people, or one of the kingdoms from another, or making any faction or parties amongst the people, contrary to the league and covenant, that they may be brought to public trial and receive condign punishment, as the degree of their offences shall require or deserve, or the supreme judicatories of both kingdoms respectively, or others having power from them for that effect, shall judge convenient.

V.

And whereas the happiness of a blessed peace between these kingdoms, denied in former times to our progenitors, is by the good providence of God granted to us, and hath been lately concluded and settled by both Parliaments: we shall each one of us, according to our places and interest, endeavour that they may remain conjoined in a firm peace and union to all posterity, and that justice may be done upon the wilful opposers thereof, in manner expressed in the precedent articles.

VI.

We shall also, according to our places and callings, in this common cause of religion, liberty and peace of the kingdom, assist and defend all those that enter into this league and covenant, in the maintaining and pursuing thereof; and shall not suffer ourselves, directly or indirectly, by whatsoever combination, persuasion or terror, to be divided and withdrawn from this blessed union and conjunction, whether to make defection to the contrary part, or give ourselves to a detestable indifferency or neutrality in this cause, which so much concerneth the glory of God, the good of the kingdoms, and the honour of the King; but shall all the days of our lives zealously and constantly continue therein, against all opposition, and promote the same according to our power, against all lets and impediments whatsoever; and what we are not able ourselves to suppress or overcome we shall reveal and make known, that it may be timely prevented or removed: all which we shall do as in the sight of God.

And because these kingdoms are guilty of many sins and provocations against God, and His Son Jesus Christ, as is too manifest by our present distresses and dangers, the fruits thereof: we profess and declare, before God and the world, our unfeigned desire to be humbled for our own sins, and for the sins of these kingdoms; especially that we have not as we ought valued the inestimable benefit of the Gospel; that we have not laboured for the purity and power thereof; and that we have not endeavoured to receive Christ in our hearts, nor to walk worthy of Him in our lives, which are the causes of other sins and transgressions so much abounding amongst us, and our true and unfeigned purpose, desire and endeavour, for ourselves and all others under our power and charge, both in public and in private, in all duties we owe to God and man, to amend our lives, and each one to go before another in the example of a real reformation, that the Lord may turn away His wrath and heavy indignation, and establish these Churches and kingdoms in truth and peace. And this covenant we make in the presence of Almighty God, the Searcher of all hearts, with a true intention to perform the same, as we shall answer at that Great Day when the secrets of all hearts shall be disclosed: most humbly beseeching the Lord to strengthen us by His Holy Spirit for this end, and to bless our desires and proceedings with such success as may be a deliverance and safety to His people, and encouragement to the Christian Churches groaning under or in danger of the yoke of Antichristian tyranny, to join in the same or like association and covenant, to the glory of God, the enlargement of the kingdom of Jesus Christ, and the peace and tranquility of Christian kingdoms and commonwealths.

Excerpted from the book, *The Constitutional Documents of the Puritan Revolution 1628-1660*. Selected and edited by Samuel Rawson Gardner. Oxford: Clarendon Press, 1889, Pages 187-190.

ABOUT THE AUTHOR

MICHAEL WAGNER is the Senior Alberta Columnist for the Western Standard and Alberta Report based in Edmonton, Alberta. He has a PhD in political science from the University of Alberta and has authored several books on Alberta politics and the independence movement. He has also authored books on Canada and its Christian heritage and religio-cultural development such as *Leaving God Behind: The Charter of Rights and Canada's Official Rejection of Christianity*, and *Standing On Guard For Thee: The Past, Present, and Future of Canada's Christian Right*. Michael and his wife and eleven children live in Edmonton, Alberta.

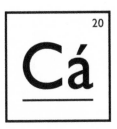

About the Cántaro Institute
Inheriting, Informing, Inspiring

The Cántaro Institute is a confessional evangelical Christian organization established in 2020 that seeks to recover the riches of historic Protestantism for the renewal and edification of the contemporary church and to advance the comprehensive Christian philosophy of life for the religious reformation of the Western and Ibero-American world.

We believe that as the Christian church returns to the fount of Scripture as her ultimate authority for all knowing and living, and wisely applies God's truth to every aspect of life, faithful in spirit to the reformers, her missiological activity will result in not only the renewal of the human person but also the reformation of culture, an inevitable result when the true scope and nature of the gospel is made known and applied.

Printed in the USA
CPSIA information can be obtained
at www.ICGtesting.com
JSHW020225100124
55125JS00003B/22